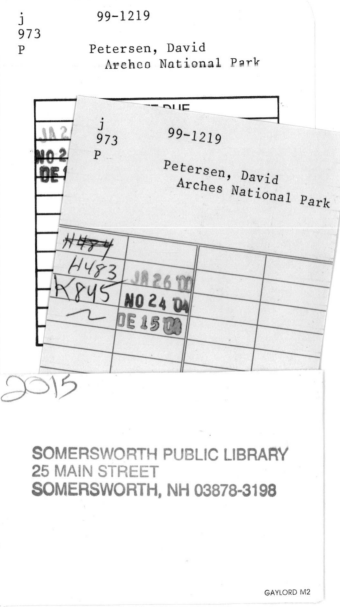

ARCHES NATIONAL PARK

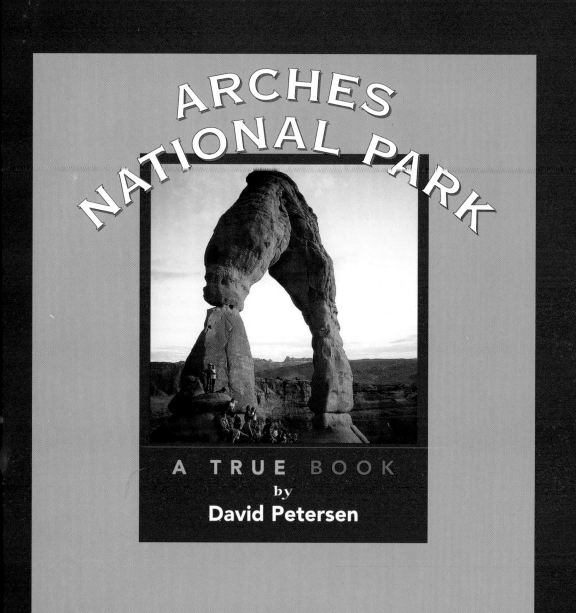

A TRUE BOOK

by
David Petersen

Children's Press®
A Division of Grolier Publishing

New York London Hong Kong Sydney
Danbury, Connecticut

A kit fox

Subject Consultant
Diane Allen
Chief of Interpretation
Arches National Park

Reading Consultant
Linda Cornwell
Coordinator of School Quality
and Professional Improvement
Indiana State Teachers
Association

**Visit Children's Press® on the
Internet at:**
http://publishing.grolier.com

Library of Congress Cataloging-in-Publication Data

Petersen, David, 1946—
    Arches National Park / by David Petersen.
        p.   cm. — (A true book)
    Includes bibliographical references and index.
    Summary: Describes the history, landscape, wildlife, and available
activities of Arches National Park.
    ISBN: 0-516-20941-8 (lib. bdg.)   0-516-26572-5 (pbk.)
    1. Arches National Park (Utah)—Juvenile literature. [1. Arches
National Park (Utah) 2. National parks and reserves.] I. Title. II. Series.
F832.A7P48   1999
979.2'58—dc21   98-42177
                                                                       CIP
                                                                       AC

© 1999 Children's Press®
a Division of Grolier Publishing Co., Inc.
All rights reserved. Published simultaneously in Canada.
Printed in the United States of America.

Contents

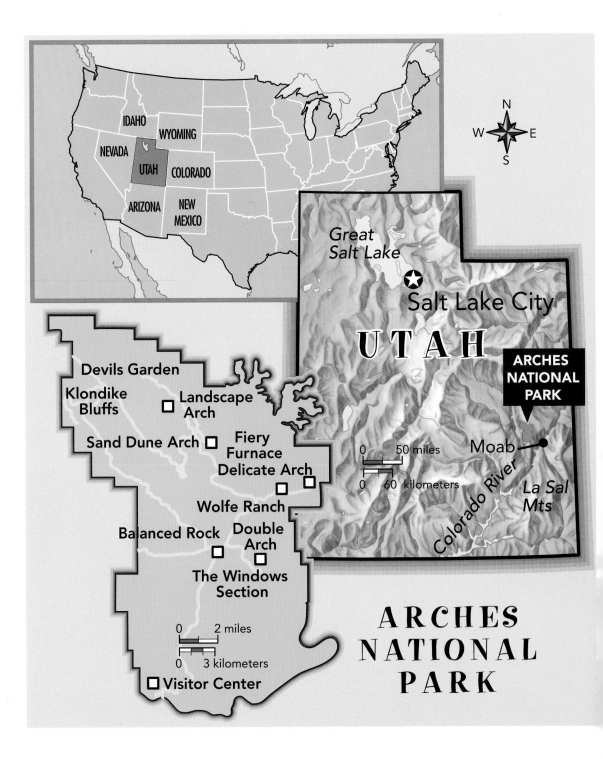

IDAHO

WYOMING

NEVADA

UTAH

COLORADO

ARIZONA

NEW
MEXICO

N
W · E
S

Great
Salt Lake

★
Salt Lake City

UTAH

ARCHES
NATIONAL
PARK

Moab

Colorado River

La Sal
Mts

0   50 miles

0   60 kilometers

Devils Garden

Klondike
Bluffs

□ Landscape
Arch

Sand Dune Arch □

Fiery
Furnace

Delicate Arch

□   □

Wolfe Ranch

Balanced Rock

Double
Arch

□   □

The Windows
Section

0   2 miles

0   3 kilometers

□ Visitor Center

ARCHES
NATIONAL
PARK

The Most Beautiful Place on Earth

Arches National Park, in southeast Utah, has been called "the most beautiful place on earth." It may be one of the strangest places, too. Arches' beauty is simple, stony, and dreamlike. It's a magical mix of rocky desert, rose-tinted cliffs, and lifelike rock formations. Arches is more than a park—it's nature's own art museum.

The country surrounding Arches National Park is special as well. Just to the southeast, between the park entrance and the town of Moab, flows the mighty Colorado River. Farther southeast, visible from many points in the park, rise the La Sal Mountains. The La Sals are

The Colorado River winds through stone canyons.

The La Sal Mountains are Utah's second-largest mountain range.

pine green in summer, aspen gold in autumn, and snow-white in winter.

The Arches story begins millions of years ago, when streams deposited thick layers of sand and silt atop the salty bed of a dry inland sea. With the help of natural calcium cements and lots of time, the sand became sandstone.

Much later, the salt layer, thousands of feet thick, shifted and settled. This fractured (broke apart) the sandstone, forming deep cracks in its surface. As hundreds of years passed, rainwater poured into the fractures in the sandstone. Little by little, mild

"The Walking Men" of Klondike Bluffs (above), and the Fiery Furnace (opposite), looking like a heap of white-hot coals.

acids in the water dissolved the calcium cements, returning sandstone to sand, one grain, one thin layer at a time. In winter, water trapped in the cracks

froze and expanded, over and
over again. This caused crum-
bling and flaking of the rock
surface, speeding the recycling
of sandstone to sand.

Over long periods of time, the cracks grew wider. The stone walls standing between the cracks were worn ever thinner. Finally they came to resemble fins—just like on a fish's back. Today, in the sections of Arches National Park called Devils Garden, Fiery Furnace, and Klondike Bluffs, hundreds of fins stand side by side. And from fins, arches are made.

The Making of an Arch

Yesterday, today, tomorrow, rain comes down and winter nights freeze. Slowly, but surely, erosion eats holes all the way through weak spots in some fins. These openings, sunlit from behind, resemble small windows in large buildings.

13

Gigantic sandstone fins are the arches of tomorrow.

As more time passes, the windows continue to erode and enlarge. Once an opening is larger than 3 feet (1 meter) across, it is considered an arch. Meanwhile, the fins containing the arches continue to wear away. Erosion is at work, from above and below. Finally, arch-shaped spans of rock, with foundations at either end, are all that remain of the fins.

A Gallery

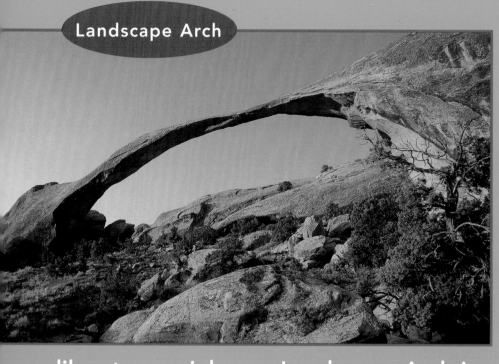

Landscape Arch

Arches come in many shapes and sizes. Some are long, thin, and graceful, like stone rainbows. Landscape Arch is an example of this, measuring 306 feet (93 m) long, but only 12 feet (3.6 m) in thickness, from top to bottom.

Other arches are more sharply bent, resembling giant, upside-down horseshoes. The most interesting of these is Delicate Arch, which balances on the shoulder of a high cliff. Double Arch,

# of Arches

in the
Windows
section of
the park,
was featured
in the movie
"Indiana
Jones and
the Last Crusade."
 Arches National
Park contains more than
two thousand natural
rock spans, from tiny
windows to arches big
enough to fly an air-
plane through.

Double Arch

Wildlife

Arches country is desert. Little rain or snow falls there most years. Summers are sizzling hot, and winters are icy cold. The air temperature on a July afternoon in the park can average almost 100° Fahrenheit (38°Celsius). The ground, baking under a fierce sun, gets even hotter. January nights average a nippy 19°F (-7°C), with occasional blizzards.

Most people visit Arches only during the pleasant seasons of spring and fall—but thousands of wild animals live there all year long. Through a slow process of change called evolution, the animals of Arches have adapted to local extremes of heat, cold, and drought.

A mule deer doe, (above). The jackrabbit, (left), makes its home in ground hollows throughout the park.

Most of Arches' thirty-eight species of mammals are nocturnal—active at night, then resting in shade through the hot summer days. That's why twilight (after sunset but before full darkness) is the best time to spot such night-loving creatures as mule deer, cottontails, and foxes.

Reptiles—lizards and snakes—thrive in the summer heat, and are easy to spot.

A longnose leopard lizard

But you won't see reptiles during winter, when they enter the long, deep sleep of hibernation.

Amphibians—frogs and toads—also hibernate in winter. In summer, look for amphibians in or near water.

Some 188 species of birds fill Arches' skies. It's hard to miss the big, noisy black ravens. Jays, swifts, swallows, and wrens are also plentiful. You might even see hawks, falcons, and eagles.

This raven (above) seems to think it's a tourist! Coyotes (right) have two howling seasons—mid-winter and early fall.

At night, listen for the spooky hooting of owls, and the howl of coyotes.

Plant Life

Like their animal neighbors, more than four hundred plant species have adapted to life in Arches country. Perfectly at home here are Utah junipers and pinyon pines. Both are small evergreen trees that need very little water. They often grow in mixed pygmy,

A juniper tree in a field of yellow-flowering rabbit brush

or small, forests. Near water, you'll see cottonwoods, willows, and other leafy trees.

Blue-green sage, yellow-flowering rabbit brush, and other bushy plants are everywhere, providing food and shelter for wildlife. You will also see thorny cacti bristle here and there, including pricklypear, whipple cholla, claret cup, and fishhook.

Grasses grow in low, moist areas and cover about 8,000 acres (3,237 hectares) of the park. In spring and early summer, the stony face of Arches is brightened by thousands of

A claret cup cactus (right) and an evening primrose (below)

wildflowers—including purple larkspur, yellow sunflowers, red-orange Indian paintbrush, blue lupine, scarlet Gilia, and dozens more.

The Crypto-Crust

Among the most important life forms at Arches is the cryptobiotic (krip-to-by-AH-tik) crust. This is a dark, bumpy "skin" covering the sand. It contains lichens, mosses, algae, bacteria, and fungi.

The cryptobiotic crust is important to the desert ecosystem. It traps precious moisture and resists water and wind erosion. It also produces nitrogen, an important plant food.

But the "crypto-crust" is very delicate and slow growing. That's why it's important to stay on the trails, washes (places where water flows), or on solid rock, when hiking at Arches.

Crust damaged by a hiker's footprint

Human Visitors

For thousands of years, American Indians visited Arches country. They came to hunt animals for food and skins, and to gather edible, or safe to eat, plants. They also collected a kind of quartz called chert. When broken, chert fractures into

Arrowheads made from chert

razor-sharp flakes that are useful as weapons and tools. White people arrived only about 150 years ago. And like the Indians before them, they rarely stayed long.

But John Wesley Wolfe, a Civil War veteran, did stay. Wolfe came to what is now Arches National Park in 1898. Beside a small creek called Salt Wash, he built a tiny cabin and spent the next twelve years there, raising cattle.

The Wolfe Ranch, located on the foot trail to Delicate Arch, has been preserved for the enjoyment of today's park visitors—and tomorrow's.

John Wolfe's cabin
as it looks today

Your own exploration of Arches National Park should begin at the visitor center. There, you'll find displays explaining the geology, or the study of earth's rocks, wildlife, plants, and human history of Arches. You can take a slide-show tour of the park, browse through the bookshop, and learn how to become an Arches Junior Ranger.

From the visitor center, the park road snakes 18 miles (29 kilometers) to Devils Garden.

Learning time spent with a park ranger will make your visit more fun.

Balanced Rock looks like a prehistoric castle from a distance.

Here it ends in Arches' only campground. Along the way, you'll pass Balanced Rock. This huge, egg-shaped rock is balanced high atop a narrow rock platform. You'll also see windows, arches, columns, viewpoints, and more. Side roads lead to even more wonders.

But the very best of Arches lies beyond the pavement, where miles of foot trails lead to dozens of hidden treasures.

Hikers near the
Devils Garden trail

For an example: Just before reaching Devils Garden campground, watch for the trail to Sand Dune Arch. At the base of Sand Dune Arch, clean sand is piled deep and steep, between the giant fins. You'll find it impossible to resist scrambling up and tumbling back down—over and over again. But remember the park ranger's warning to never jump off or climb on the arch itself.

Shady Sand Dune Arch provides a welcome sandbox break.

Shaded most of the day by
the sky-scraping fins on
either side, Sand Dune Arch
is a really cool place for kids!

For All People, for All Time

To preserve the natural wonders of Arches, President Herbert Hoover created a small national monument in 1929. Later presidents enlarged the monument to its present size of 114 square miles (295 sq km). And in 1971, Congress made Arches a national park.

Animals, birds, the American West's greatest river, snow-capped mountain peaks, a rose-tinted desert haunted by weird, wonderful sandstone sculptures: This is Arches National Park, Utah—one of the most beautiful places on earth.

Red-glowing stone formations give
the park its strange beauty.

To Find Out More

Here are some additional resources to help you learn more about Arches National Park:

 **Books**

Anderson, Alan. **Geology Crafts for Kids: 50 Nifty Projects to Explore the Marvels of Planet Earth.** Sterling, 1996.

Howell, Catherine H. **Reptiles and Amphibians.** National Geographic, 1994.

Landau, Elaine. **Desert Mammals.** Children's Press, 1996.

Lye, Keith. **Rocks and Minerals.** Raintree Steck-Vaughn, 1994.

Thompson, Katherine. **Utah.** Raintree Steck-Vaughn, 1996.

American Park Network
http://www.americanpark network.com/parkinfo/ar

Visitor information, tips for photographers, and "The Electronic Campfire" featuring discussion groups. Click on other national park sites, from Acadia to Zion.

Arches National Park
3031 South Highway 191
Moab, UT 84532
http://www.arches.national park.com

Canyonlands Natural History Association
30 South 100 East
Moab, UT 84532

Great Outdoor Recreation Pages (GORP)
http://www.gorp.com/ resource/US_National_Park /ut_arche.htm

Information on hiking and bike trails, camping, plant life, wildlife, and more.

National Park Service
2282 S. West Resource Blvd.
Moab, UT 84532
http://www.nps.gov

General information on all of the national parks.

45

Important Words

blizzard a fierce, wind-driven snowstorm

drought long periods of time without rain or snow

ecosystem a local community of living and non-living things, each of which depends upon the others

erosion to wear away by the action of water or wind

fungus a plant, such as a mold or a mushroom, that grows in dark, moist places (plural: fungi)

lichen a plant system made up of fungus and many tiny one-celled plants, which grows on a solid surface such as rock

recycle to return to an original or earlier condition

silt fine earth combined with tiny rock particles, deposited by water or wind

span space or distance between two places

Index

Meet the Author

David Petersen lives with his wife, Caroline, and their two dogs in a cabin in Colorado, a half day from Arches National Park. David has written more than two dozen titles for Children's Press. His most recent "big kids" book is *The Nearby Faraway: A Personal Journey Through the Heart of the West* (Johnson Books). His True Books on America's national parks include *Bryce Canyon, Great Sand Dunes, Petrified Forest,* and *Saguaro.*

Photographs ©: Branson Reynolds: 2, 11, 14, 17 bottom, 20 top, 25, 27, 28, 29, 31, 35, 36; Donald Young: 1, 10, 33, 40; Kathleen Norris Cook: 43; Peter Arnold Inc.: 23 bottom (Gerard Lacz), 8 (Richard Weiss), cover (John Wieffer); Tom Bean: 7, 16, 38; Tony Stone Images: 17 top (David Barnes), 23 top (John Elk), 20 bottom (John Perret), 21 (Rod Planck).

Map by Joe LeMonnier.